in the Name of the Most Compassionate,
Ever Compassionate Allah

The Doctrine
of Polygyny

Mojtaba Khosravi khah
Translator: Sarah Nosrati
August 2015

نویسنده : مجتبی خسروی خواه
شابک : ۵-۱۵۱۰-۰۴-۶۰۰-۹۷۸
رده بندی دیویی : ۲۹۷/۴۸۳۱
شماره کتابشناسی ملی : ۳۵۹۵۱۹۸

Title: The Doctrine of Polygyny

Author: Mojtaba Khosravi Khah

Translator: Sarah Nosrati

Editor: Hamed Khosro Abadi

ISBN-13: 978-1939123077

LCCN: 2015905118

Publicator: Supreme Century, 2015

Mojtaba_Khosravikhah@yahoo.com

Price: 10$

Contents

Contents

Contents

The Doctrine of Polygyny

Introduction

Every day, human beings see many groupings, each of which has a series of input and output components. It is argued that one of the main points of these groupings is the necessity of establishing a balance among the input components. Since violating this condition might lead to not only the loss of input sources and its cost, but also it would have a negative impact on the output.

Therefore, to avoid the harmful consequences of this imbalance, it is necessary to control the amount of components in proportion to each other and prevent their excessive entry into the grouping.

For example, if in cooking (the grouping), salt (the input component) is overused in proportion to the other ingredients, the food (the output component) will be inedible. By controlling the amount of salt, one can avoid wasting raw materials as well as cooking bad tasting food.

In contrast to the above set in which the components' entry and control are done in a short time, there are some other groupings in which the components' entry is consecutive; as a result, they require continuous monitoring.

Marriage is one of these groupings in which the men and women who are ready to marry are considered as inputs, and the married individuals are regarded as outputs. Given the important principle of proportionality between input components, it is evident that the establishment of balance between the number of men and women when they enter the marriage arena has special significance; lacking which may definitely cause many difficulties.

Hence, this book initially investigates whether there is a balance between the input components, i.e., the men and the women who are ready to marry; if not, what is the reason and how long this imbalance would continue?

Then, it probes into the question of how the harmful consequences of this imbalance would be reflected in the society. Finally, what solutions can be offered to act as a controller? So that, in addition to preventing the cost of the marriage input components' loss, it would act as a protection for marriage system outputs (the married individuals).

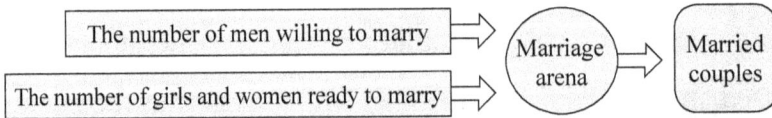

The number of men willing to marry	⟹	Marriage arena	⟹	Married couples
The number of girls and women ready to marry	⟹			

Figure 1

Chapter 1:
The Main Cause of the Permanent Higher Number of Girls and Single Women

Given the fact that the existence of proportionality between the input components is one of the main points regarding the health of the groupings, it can be asserted that the best possible state for marriage may be achieved through establishing continuous balance and equality between the two groups of single men qualified for marriage and the single women willing to marry.

However, this ideal state would never occur due to the changes caused by the effect of various quantitative and qualitative factors. The factors violating the above-mentioned balance include migration, sex ratio at birth and death, war and conflict, physical and emotional problems, economic issues, etc.

One of the most important factors emerges through the combination of the marriage age gap with population growth which will be discussed as follows:

Marriage Age gap:

With regard to the men and women's age at the time of marriage, three general age gaps would be considered for couples:

1-Positive age gap: The man is older than the woman;

2-Zero age gaps: The man is as old as the woman (the same-age);

3-Negative age gap: The man is younger than the woman.

Population Growth:

With reference to a certain time period, we can consider three states for population growth. If the above-mentioned time period is one year, then we have:

1-Positive population growth: the number of births per year is higher than that of the previous year.

2-Zero population growth: the number of births per year is equal to that of the previous year.

3-Negative population growth: the number of births per year is less than that of the previous year.

It is clearly seen that in the marriages taking place in the world, the average age of the men is higher than the women's age and also the population growth in the world has been always increasing, i.e. we have had positive population growth.

Population growth of the world:	Positive ○	Zero ○	Negative ○
Average marriage age gap:	Positive ○	Zero ○	Negative ○

The Combination of Positive Marriage Age gap with Positive Population Growth:

As discussed earlier, the best balancing state in marriage would occur only when there is balance between the proportion of the number of men and women seeking to marry. However, the combination of these two factors, i.e. positive population growth and positive marriage age gap can disturb this balance and a number of women would permanently remain as surplus single women in the society.

To clarify this point, we exemplify it by assuming a set with zero initial population. Firstly, in this set, the number of male and female individuals born per year is equal; and secondly, the population growth is positive (the number of the male or female born per year is one person more than the previous year).

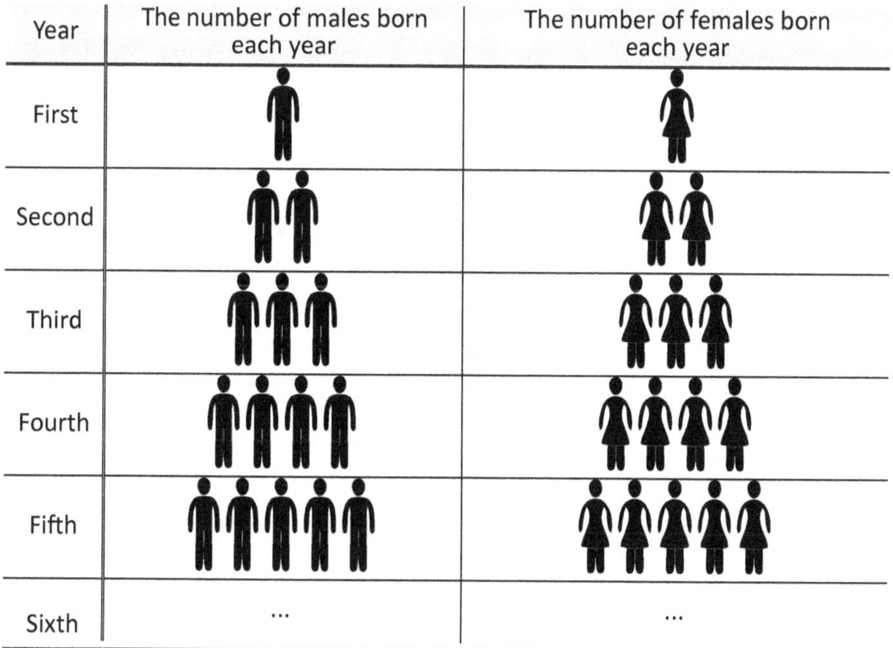

Year	The number of males born each year	The number of females born each year
First	♂ (1)	♀ (1)
Second	♂♂ (2)	♀♀ (2)
Third	♂♂♂ (3)	♀♀♀ (3)
Fourth	♂♂♂♂ (4)	♀♀♀♀ (4)
Fifth	♂♂♂♂♂ (5)	♀♀♀♀♀ (5)
Sixth	...	...

Figure 2: An Instance of Positive Population Growth

The first state: in the aforementioned set, if a man from the first year wants to marry a woman who is of the same age with him, among the women of the group, there is only one option (woman) who is of the same age with him (Figure 3).

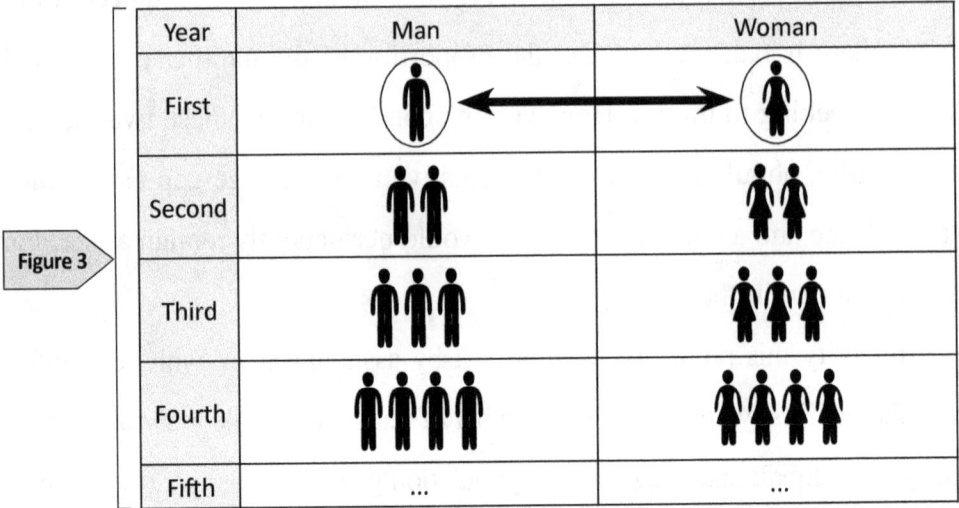

Figure 3

Year	Man	Woman
First		
Second		
Third		
Fourth		
Fifth	...	...

Moreover, for the two men from the second year, there are only two options (women) for marriage that are of the same age with those two men and so on (figure 4)

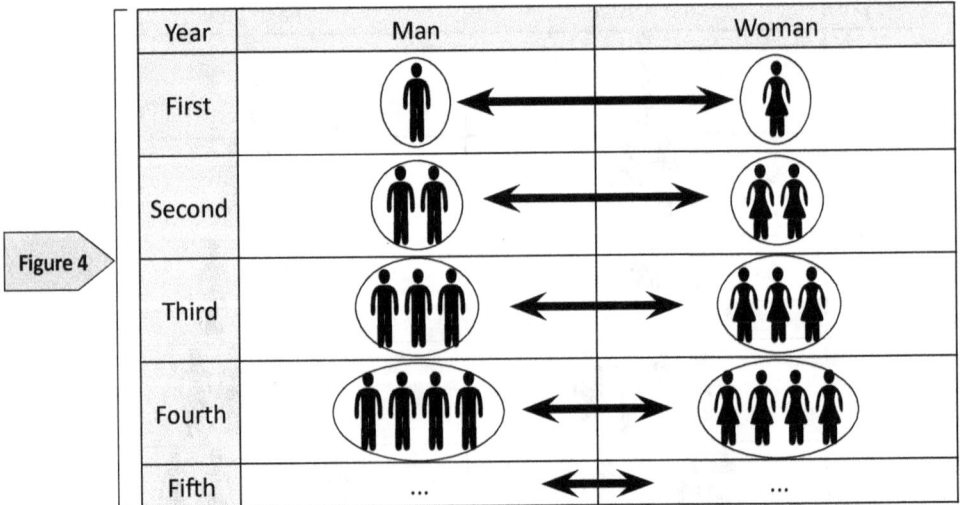

Figure 4

Year	Man	Woman
First		
Second		
Third		
Fourth		
Fifth	...	...

Thus, when the same-age marriage becomes conventional, then every year there would be an equal number of these two groups of men and women, and no man or woman would remain single.

The second state: but if a man from the first year wants to marry a woman who is one year younger than him, among the women of the group there would be two options (women) for marriage with one of whom he marries and the other one would remain as the surplus single woman in the group (Figure 5).

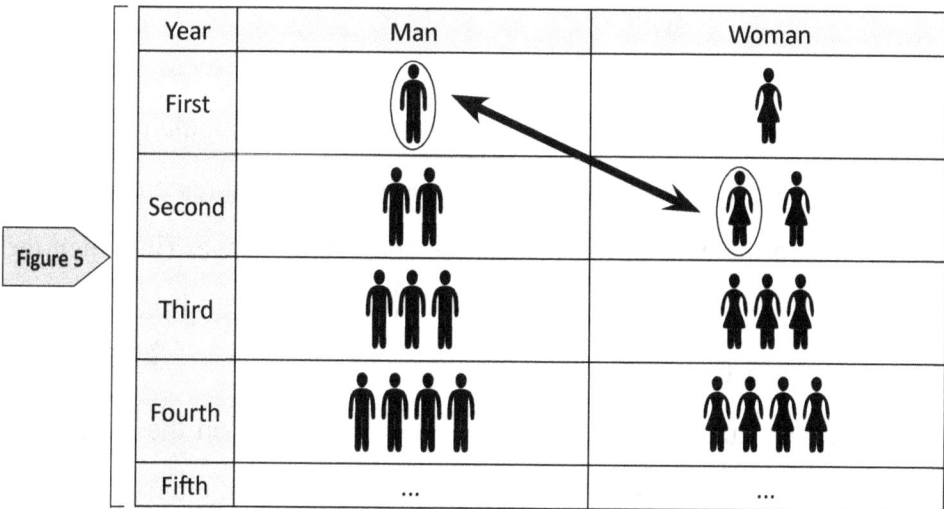

Figure 5

Year	Man	Woman
First		
Second		
Third		
Fourth		
Fifth	...	...

Also for the two men from the second year, there would be three options (women who are one year younger than them), two of them would marry and one option would remain single, and so on (figure 6)

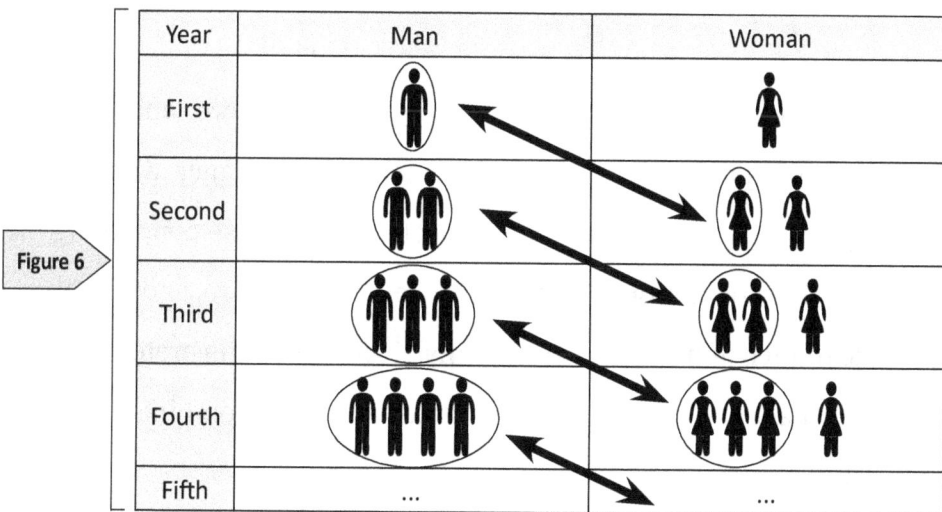

Figure 6

Year	Man	Woman
First		
Second		
Third		
Fourth		
Fifth	...	...

Thus, it can be said that by convention of the one-year age gap in marriage, each year, one woman would remain as surplus single in this set.

***

Generally and with regard to the above example, for a set as large as the society it can be concluded that in the state of positive population growth, and the approximate equality of the number of males and females born per year, and also the convention of positive age gap marriages (in which the highest percentage of marriages is related to the marriage of the men with women younger than themselves)…

…since the number of men born each year is less than the number of women born in subsequent years, some women will remain as surplus single ones in the society annually with no husband for them (see figure 6).

Obviously, with an increase in the slope of population growth and also in the average gap between the couple's age, the number of women who will remain as surplus singles per year will go up, too.

In sum, and with regard to the average positive, zero, and negative marriage age gap (in which the men marry the younger women, the same-age women or older women respectively) and also concerning the three possible population growth states (i.e. positive, zero, and negative), the state of men and women seeking marriage can be illustrated in cases of the permanency of each of these states and their combinations with each other:

Table 1: Results of the permanent combination of marriage age gap (positive, zero, and negative) with population growth (positive, zero, and negative)			
Population Growth \ Age gap	Positive (Man is older than woman)	Zero (Man is as old as woman)	Negative (Man is younger than woman)
Positive	A: a surplus of women	B:Balanced	C: a surplus of men
Zero	D: Balanced	E:Balanced	F: Balanced
Negative	G: a surplus of men	H: Balanced	I: a surplus of women

As table 1 depicts, the probability of establishing a balance between the men and the women who are ready to marry is possible only in two states:

1- When the population growth is always zero (Table 1: F, E, D); and/or

2- When the zero marriage age gap (the same-age marriages) becomes a convention in the society permanently (Table 1: H, E, B).

Otherwise, the equality ratio of the men and the women who are ready to marry will be lost.

It should be noted that, although, these two options may seem practical solutions for establishing a balance; indeed, they were considered inefficient overtime and could not provide appropriate solutions for striking a balance; because they were not in line with human beings' wants, and were more detrimental than beneficial.

For example, population growth may be zero or even negative in certain periods of time (permanent negative population growth would lead to the extinction of humankind). However, due to various innate drives such as achieving welfare, convenience, progress, etc, (all of which originate from the existence of young human forces), the population growth has always been positive over time (and throughout history).

Furthermore, the disadvantages of conventionalization of the same-age marriage are as follows:

1-Very long waiting time for marriage would dominate the women's community.

2-The minimum marriage age for girls would be simultaneous with the beginning of puberty age in boys, meaning that the probability of girls marrying before the puberty age in boys is zero.

3-It is possible that some percentages of marriages occur in the form of the same-age marriages or even the woman be older than the man; still the majority of men and women prefer the man to be older than the woman for better matching of physical and emotional conditions.

4-At last, this option would be useful in establishing the balance only when from the very beginning, the same-age marriages could occur permanently and there were no surplus single women in the society. (i.e. the society did not tend toward the same-age marriages as an inevitable option and due to the men's reduced population).

In summary, with regard to the above mentioned fact and the following ones:

1-Permanency of positive population growth overtime and

2- Higher percentage of marriages with positive age gap in which the man is older than the woman

From the combination of these two, it can be concluded that:

> In the marriages occurring in the society and the world, every year a number of single women would remain as the surplus; and this would lead to permanent increase in the number of girls and women ready to marry over that of the men throughout the world. (Appendix 1).

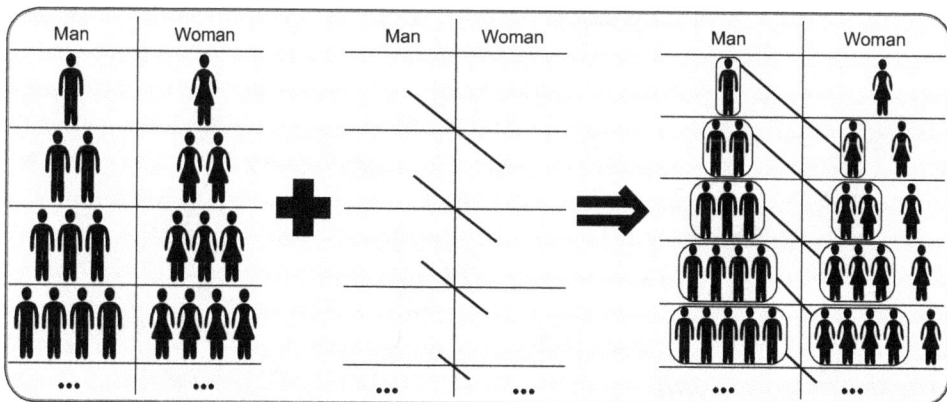

Chapter 2:

Nature's Solutions for Controlling the Surplus Singles

(difference in creation of the man and woman)

As it was shown in the previous chapter, due to the combination of marriage age gap with population growth, the balance between the proportions of the number of men to women seeking marriage would be upset leading to the emergence of some surplus single people who should remain as reserve in the society.

It should be noted that despite the impossibility of preventing this phenomenon, the system of the universe has been created in such a way that provides natural solutions to neutralize this imbalance, so that the resultant problems can be solved and the balance be reestablished.

We know that it is possible that the imbalance between the supply and demand for marriage to occur in the two following ways:

1-Higher number of men seeking marriage in comparison to women (demand greater than supply)

2-Higher number of women seeking marriage in comparison to men (supply more than demand)

Considering the permanent positive population growth over time and the higher percentages of marriages in which the men are older than the women, it is certain that over time the state (2) will occur in the world. But because of the possibility of state (1) occurring in some places and for short whiles, the following conditions will arise, for which the natural solutions for returning to the state of balance are investigated.

Higher Number of Men Seeking Marriage in Comparison to Women:

In this condition, first, the women within the conventional marriage age would marry and exit the supply set. Then, when the women in this group are finished, some men seeking marriage will remain with no spouse.

This will influence the men's taste criteria which act as a filter and limiting factor in their selection of women. Therefore, these criteria will gradually disappear and be ignored by them; the most important of these criteria is the women's age.

Hence, by marriage and reduction in the number of single women who are within the conventional marriage age range, the remaining men, who are in search of a spouse for themselves, would go for the women whose age is younger than this range.

So, all the single girls and women whose age is between the puberty age and the conventional marriage age will be the new female members ready to marry, and the capacity of the supply set would be enhanced.

Certainly, the longer the time period in which the number of men is higher than the number of women, the more the girls and single women will marry and exit the supply set. Thus, the reduction and decline in the number of girls and single women, and their marriage age can be the main indication of a relative increase in the number of men seeking marriage over that of the women in the society.

Therefore, it can be said that in the first stage, the problem of higher number of men seeking marriage compared to women has been resolved through gradual decrease in the marriage age of the women. These changes will continue until the balance between demand and supply in marriage is reestablished.

***

In the second stage, if there is a continual rise in the number of men to women, and the single women's and girls' supply reaches its full capacity, then,, this would lead to the condition that the men, due to physical possessiveness in their nature (which brings for them the acquisition and maintenance of territorial possession), coupled with their intrinsic needs and desires, gradually will gravitate towards the only possible option, i.e. the married women.

This issue, on the one hand, is in sharp contrast to the emotional belongingness in the female's nature (who likes to be married to only one husband and belong to one man); and on the other hand, it is incompatible with the married men's physical possessiveness characteristic of strongly trying to keep their territory.

Therefore, by interference and confrontation of the two males' physical possessiveness forces with each other_ one seeking to acquire the territorial possession and the other trying to maintain his territorial possession _, both of them would try their best for certain and permanent physical repulsion of the other. This aim can only be achieved in two ways:

1- Separation: one of them must accept to leave the territory of the other and distance himself from it, so that in this way, the probability of affecting and invading individual privacy is minimized as much as possible.

2-Elimination: a hard battle (and war, in a larger scale) to achieve one's own goals and desires which would lead to the death of one party.

It is predictable that at first, due to the small number of surplus single men, repulsion practices are more likely to occur through separation rather than repulsion by elimination. However, by increase in the number of single men and also due to the existence of the motive for acquiring the possession in them, the possibility of confrontation and occurrence of repulsion practices through elimination would be strongly enhanced.

***

As it can be seen, human beings have been created in such a way that initially the problem of higher number of men could be solved as much as possible and the balance be kept by making some changes in age gap and reducing the women's marriage age. Then, if the problem of surplus men continues, the creation system reestablishes the balance by eliminating them via putting the inherent physical possessiveness trait in male beings.

***

Whilst, naturally there are secondary solutions (i.e. repulsion or elimination) for solving this problem, it is clear-cut that creating a number of human beings without meeting their needs is somewhat in contrast with the organized nature of the creation system.

Therefore, prior to the rise of the process of men's physical possessiveness confrontation which would lead to their separation or elimination, a third natural option _, considered as the most important factor in preventing the formation of the surplus males_, will be activated in them; i.e. the human beings' innate desire for reproducing and multiplying to achieve more progress and prosperity as well as to avoid permanent reduction and extinction.

Consequently, with the impact of this natural factor, the main reason for surplus men, which results from the combination of negative population growth with positive marriage age gap (Table 1: G), would no longer have any effect.

***

In sum, it can be stated that although it is possible that the factor of negative population growth (which lead to the relative increase in the number of men compared to women) may be generated in a small location during a short while, in the long run it would never be able to influence a great area i.e. the whole earth permanently.

Higher Number of Women Seeking Marriage in Comparison to Men:

As mentioned earlier, the strongest factor creating this condition is the combination of positive population growth with the positive marriage age gap. Firstly, the equality between demand and supply, leads to a situation in which there would be one woman for each man seeking marriage; in this case the probability of marriage for each woman is one hundred percent. But over time and due to a combination of conditions leading to an increase in the ratio of the number of women to men, more women will enter the marriage arena than men seeking marriage in a certain time span.

Then, due to the above-mentioned fact, of the total number of women, some of them would remain single and be kept in the supply set as surplus members. In the next time span, with the entrance of a new series of women and men seeking marriage, new men would choose a wife from the two groups of women:

1- The new women who have entered into the marriage demand and supply system simultaneously with those men.

2-The women who have been reserved in the supply set from the previous year or years.

Generally, in order to have more compatibility with the popular convention, most marriages occur according to the dominant age gap in the society; and this would decrease the probability of being chosen from among the women remaining from the former years than the new women.

Although this difference in the probability of being chosen exists, the second group of women still have the chance of being selected and in reality some of them will marry.

Therefore, as a result of exchanging some members of these two groups in the marital arena, the preceding period women will marry at the cost of unwanted postponement in the marriage of the new women entrants (to the marriage arena); so the new women entrants themselves would be turned into the surplus women.

Furthermore, by increase in the marriages of the surplus women whose age is higher than the conventional marriage age, slowly but surely the total average marriage age in women and girls would also increase.

It should be noted that even though postponement in the marriage of new women entrants is helpful and can act as a compensation for marriage of the women remaining from the previous group, and can to some extent solve the problem of the higher number of women seeking marriage than that of men, this matter has time and conventional limitations.

Being such, with the increase in the marriage age of women due to these exchanges, and with the marriage age gaps reaching the critical point (i.e. the same-age), not only will the number of marriages in which the women are older than men increase, but also the high percentage of single women and girls will be more evident in the society.

***

It is clear that the continuation of this trend will gradually enhance the possibility of the single women's orientation towards the married men; the greater the number of single women in the society, the higher would be the aforementioned possibility.

Here, on the contrary to the creation of males who due to their physical possessiveness nature, would try hard to acquire and keep their territory, the nature of females has not been created with these characteristics and they don't behave in such a way.

Hence, with the increased number of single women and the lack of physical possessiveness trait in their nature, neither do the single women seek to confront the married women and eliminate them to obtain a husband; nor would the married women actively try to completely repulse the single women in order to keep their husbands.

As a result, the phenomenon of certain and permanent repulsion through separation and/or elimination would not occur in the female community, even though it could be an effective option for solving the problem of the increase in the number of surplus single women.

***

It is obvious that the inefficacy of the option of an increase in the women's marriage age (that could be helpful for the problem of an annual emergence of surplus single women only for a limited time), and also the lack of certain repulsion state among the females, as well as continuation of the conditions for positive population growth over time, all would make for the continuation of the state of relative increase in the number of surplus single women in the society, being problematic directly or indirectly.

Hence, if there were no more natural alternatives to resolve this problem, then, certainly the creation system would be considered as flawed; because a number of human beings have been created with a series of needs with no possibility of being met.

Undoubtedly, envisaging this matter is in conflict with the knowledge and wisdom of God; and surely He has considered another option in nature for this problem. That option is the difference between the creation type of male and female and also the creation of men based on physical possessiveness characteristic.

So that while being a married man, psychologically and physically he has the tendency to accept another woman and not reject her (Philogyny), in order that through this, there would be a natural controlling factor for the conditions of surplus single girls and women.

Therefore, if like the female gender whose heartfelt desire is to belong and be committed to only one man, the male gender, too, would be oriented towards just one woman not accepting any other woman, then the creation would be flawed.

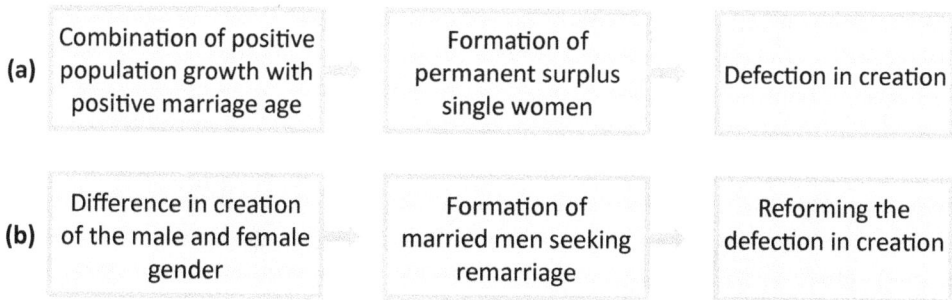

(a)	Combination of positive population growth with positive marriage age	Formation of permanent surplus single women	Defection in creation
(b)	Difference in creation of the male and female gender	Formation of married men seeking remarriage	Reforming the defection in creation

Chapter 3:
Seeking Permission from the Married Women

As it was stated previously, most of the times, there has been an imbalance between the number of men and women seeking marriage, leading to the formation of surplus singles in women. Lack of appropriate solutions not only creates individual problems in them, but also would cause some social challenges.

On the other hand, the only natural solution to this problem is the men's physical possessiveness nature and their philogyny by which and with emergence of married men seeking re-marriage, the expansion of the single surplus women's set could be prevented.

However, it is argued that men's philogyny can act as an appropriate opportunity helping to solve the problem. Yet it is inefficient in reducing the number of surplus single women due to two legal issues between husband and wife. Therefore, to change the aforementioned opportunity to a useful and applied state, firstly, two legal issues must be examined and resolved. They include:

1-Accepting the husband's relationship: A woman inherently seeks emotional possession and exclusive seizing of a man's heart; she wants her husband to give all his attention to her. This causes a married woman to prefer her personal interests to the interests of women's set and reject her husbands' relationship.

Hence, the first step in the process of preventing the expansion of single surplus women's set is that a married woman must legally recognize the issue of sharing her husband with another single woman, considering it as a legal right of another single woman; and she should be committed to accept it.

2- Accepting the required time: a married man's romantic relationship with a single woman in a limited and short period of time cannot be the only factor in removing the single surplus women from the reserved state. Therefore, the man's philogyny must be directed towards permanent attraction of the girls and single women so that by exiting them from the supply set, the creation of surplus women would be prevented.

Consequently, to achieve this purpose, the married women must accept the required sharing time so that a married man benefiting the features such as having more time or being a permanent supporter can be regarded as a husband for a single woman, too.

Accordingly, by means of these two solutions, at first, the single women and girls would be removed from the supply set by permanent marriage as much as possible. In case of the absence of required conditions for permanent marriage and remaining of some percentage of them, short-term relationships (temporary marriage) can meet the needs of the rest of them.

***

It should be noted that regarding the issue of married women's giving the right of husband-sharing to single women, since the identity of the single woman is not known and typically any single woman can be the recipient of this right, thus, declaring this commitment (i.e. the married woman's commitment to accept and give the aforementioned right to single women) and discussing it with every one of those single women is impossible.

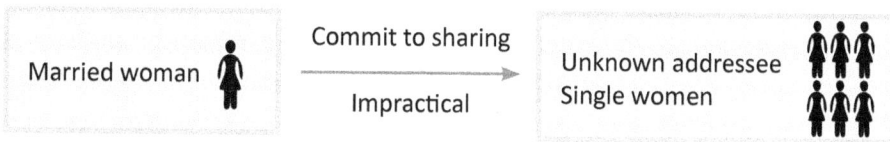

Married woman	Commit to sharing → Impractical	Unknown addressee Single women

Here we can do something which is equivalent with the above mentioned task which was impossible. I.e. instead of "giving the husband-sharing right to single woman" whose identity is unknown, we can bring up the issue of married women's "giving permission to the husband to have relations with the single woman" in which the addressee is the husband who is a known individual.

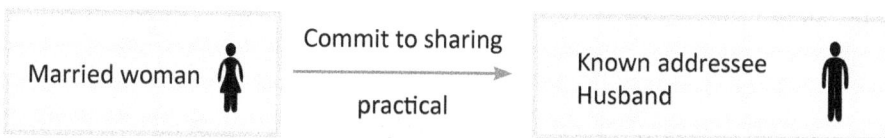

Married woman	Commit to sharing → practical	Known addressee Husband

Thus, it would be possible to reach an agreement and commitment between the husband and his wife whereby the married woman commits to recognize giving the right of husband-sharing for single women to her husband. It is evident that the most appropriate occasion for this commitment is at the time of marriage when the legal issues are discussed between the husband and wife and the woman has the option of pronouncing her acceptance

Agreed Legal Bases in Marriage:

We know that the marriage is an agreed legal contract between the man and woman which determines the duties and authorities of the couples in marital life. In negotiating a contract and defining the duties and authorities, each party is allowed to include his/her wants in it provided that the other party accepts those wants.

Furthermore, it is possible that the man or woman include some conditions that are to detriment of the other party. Hence, in order to avoid such harm, the two following solutions are offered to make agreement between the couples:

1- Equality basis: regardless of the gender differences between male and female, the nature and capabilities of the man and woman must be considered as equal whereby all legal concerns interacted in the common life are considered equally.

2- Divine basis: Due to the physical and emotional differences leading to different abilities in male and female genders, all rights may not be divided equally. However, to avoid the sense of harm in the parties, both of them should disregard their personal tastes while determining their rights, and by reference to the divine resources and religions, identify their and the other party's duties and authorities and acknowledge them.

Equality Culture:

As concerns the literal meaning of the concept 'equality', it is clear that in this pattern the basis is such that the man and woman have equal rights in all of their common authorities and responsibilities related to the affairs of their married life.

Both of them have accepted this view as dominant culture of the society and have committed themselves to observe it. This legal equality includes the issues related to a largest set i.e. the country down to the smallest one i.e. family.

For instance, since in every set, it is necessary to determine someone as the manager, in macro issues of the country either the men or women can be appointed in top positions, and accountability for social security is within the responsibilities of both genders. Concerning other matters, such as inheritance, blood money, etc the determined amount would be the same for both genders of male and female.

It is the case with the family set, too. I.e. all authorities and duties of both parties are equal from the very moment from the beginning to the end. For example, in the family set, the woman is an autonomous and independent individual with complete divorce rights just as the man. Furthermore, from the very beginning of common life, all financial responsibilities (e.g., housing and life appliances, celebrations, living expenses, sharing of the properties acquired during marital life at the time of getting a divorce, etc.) are considered within the duties of both man and woman.

All in all, both male and female genders must enjoy the same rights in all the life affairs from the trivial up to important ones, so that the parties feel no harm.

***

In this culture, one of the agreed issues between the wife and husband is that after marriage the man is committed to his wife and can only have a romantic relationship with her and vice versa.

Therefore, if a man, who has recognized the rights of his wife and committed to observe them, wants to have a romantic relationship with another woman, then he is to be considered an adulterer; this man has contravened his commitments and ignored the legal equality basis, and by doing so he has done harm to his wife.

With regard to the aforementioned discussion, obviously in equality culture it is impossible to make use of the men's physical possessiveness opportunity and their philogyny in order to solve the problem of surplus single women. Hence, in societies which accept the equality as the dominant cultural basis, the surplus single women's problems will remain unsolved.

Divine Culture (Islam):

As it was mentioned earlier, one of the principal bases accepted by men and women is to resort to the divine basis which is used for determination and classification of the rights between the men and women.

Both parties have acknowledged this basis because both of them acknowledge that the God is human being's Creator and is well aware of the features, abilities, and individual and social needs of the two genders of male and female.

Since, Islam is the last religion in which all the issues related to mankind have been comprehensively stated under the guidance of the Quran and Tradition (The Prophet Muhammad (P.B.U.H) and infallible Imams (A.S)), it is the best option among the divine religions to use for the clarification of legal issues like marriage.

In contrast to the equality culture which considers equal marital rights for the couple, in Islamic culture, the rights of the husband and the wife are completely different from each other; this is due to taking into account the difference in the genders' nature. In summary, it can be said that the most significant duties and authorities that Islam has assigned to the husband and wife are as follows:

The wife's Right:

1- Clothing;

2- Providing the Food;

3- Housing;

4- Accomodation (whether as a husband or a father);

In legal terms, these four tasks are called the alimony right.

5- Remuneration (the money a wife can request from the husband for doing every work (excluded obedience from the husband));

6- Dowry

The husband's Right:

1- If the husband wants to have a child, the wife should obey;

2- She needs the husband's consent to go out of the house;

3- The wife must meet the husband's sexual needs;

These three tasks are called the obedience right in the legal terms.

4- Divorce right;

5- The right of polygyny if provided that he has the qualifications.

Therefore, a man and a woman who marry based on the Islamic culture are familiar with the legal duties and authorities of the Muslim man and woman in the family system and have accepted them; commitment to which will be accomplished through expressing their consent during marriage vows by both parties.

One considerable fact is that contrary to the equality culture, Islam has paid attention to the subject of woman and her needs and also the individual and social harms that may occur in case that those needs are unfulfilled.

So that to achieve the goal of reform and fulfillment of their needs, the legislator has granted the permission of "being the other wife" as a right for single women, and has considered it within the man's authorities (under the title of polygyny).

In other words, in divine culture of Islam (and other religions) this acts as a type of marriage insurance for all single women to apply it in the case of need.

Duty of paying the marriage premium is within the responsibilities of the women seeking to benefit from the Muslim woman's marital rights through marrying based on the Islamic model, as they have understood the advantages and merits like women not having financial responsibility in the married life, etc.

Indeed, this payment is in the form of the wife's accepting the fact that there comes some moments in the common life that the husband does not merely and exclusively belong to her; rather he may be shared by another single woman.

Moreover, the amount of this cost has not been considered as equal for all the married women; and to establish the justice the index of "benefiting from the economic prosperity and financial ability of the husband" is used. It means that _figuratively speaking _any married women having a more financially capable husband must pay more tax in comparison to other married women if required, and accept longer husband sharing time.

In this way, by considering the right of polygyny as one of the men's authorities, Islam has optimized the physical possessiveness nature of men and their pilogyny; and by facilitating the permanent marriage of the girls and single women to qualified married men, has provided the conditions for their exit from the surplus set.

Moreover, in the absence of conditions for permanent marriage of all and remaining of some percent of the women, by supporting and giving the right of temporary marriage, Islam has prevented the total depravity of the rest of them.

It is obvious that paying the cost of the premium for the single women's marriage, either in the form of permanent or temporary marriage, is a kind of Haq – Al-Nas[1] that the married women are obliged to commit to pay at the moment of marriage.

***

It should be noted that although women have freedom of choice to accept or reject marriage according to the Islamic pattern which has been considered for women, and there is no compulsion, the critical point is that after choosing the Islamic life style which includes the necessity of their accepting polygyny, they must adhere to it practically in order to prevent the problems arising from the absence of polygyny in the society.

---

1. In Islam it refers to the mankind's right.

Chapter 4:
the Negative Consequences of not implementing the Polygyny in Society

Human beings' needs directly affect their growth and accomplishment and they must be met on time. Otherwise, they may cause physical and mental problems. Hence, human nature is such that once the signs of need start to show and are received within them, their calmness disappears and they try to find a way to meet those needs.

Women's Needs:

The fact that over time, the increase in the number of women ready to marry in comparison to that of men is an inevitable matter, has led to annual increase in the number of women who cannot marry and their needs would not be met.

Furthermore, since human nature is such that with the beginning of the desires, they make all their attempts to fulfill them. Thus, the aforementioned girls and women try to exit from the stationary state and find a way for fulfilling their needs; by doing so, they will produce some effects on the external environment or society. In brief, these needs and desires are:

- Emotional desire (to love and to be loved);
- he need for fellowship and not being alone;
- Sexual desire;
- The need to gain independence from the family;
- Financial need (particularly if she is affording the expenses of the family);
- The need to have an assistant in doing the routine works;
- The need for surviving, having children and loving them;
- The need to have a sense of being effective and busy with family affairs (Taking care of the child, loving the husband, and housekeeping)
- The need to have the social credit of being married

Troubles of relative increase in the number of girls and single women:

After choosing the Islamic pattern which requires accepting the polygyny by women, the important point is that they should conform to these commitments in practical terms, too. But, if despite the increased number of girls and women ready to marry, the married women ignore the aforementioned issue and no attempts are taken to implement and conventionalize the polygyny in society, then the ground would be paved for formation of a number of individual and social problems; some of which have been referred to as follows:

1 - The epidemic increase in the average marriage age of the female gender in society: change and replacement of the single women remaining from yesteryear or years with the single women, who are within the range of conventional marriage age, leads to a universal increase in "Women's and girls' waiting time for marriage". So, with the passing of time, the marriage age of the girls and women in society will go up and gradually the greater percent of the marriages will be related to the marriages in which the man and woman are the same age (the same-age) or even the women is older than the man.

2 – Being single for a life time: as regards the single women from the previous period, we should say that some percent of them get the chance of being replaced and marry. However, in parallel with these replacements, some percent of other women, will lose the chance of marrying and will remain single throughout their life time. Especially, by entering the critical range of the same-age marriage and regarding the resistance to higher age of the woman than man, the visibility of these single woman becomes more outstanding in the society (formerly, changes in age gap and increase in marriage age of the women, was the factor which had obscured the emergence of annual surplus women in the society). It is obvious that by population growth and the passing of each year, there will be a permanent increase in the number of these people; and all accept that depending on their chance, some of women should remain unmarried for a long time or even throughout their whole life.

3- Pre-marriage romantic relationships: the higher the probability of marriage and the less the waiting time for marriage, the higher is the "the hope to marry in the near future" in girls mentality and vice versa.

In other words, the lower the conventional marriage age for the female gender in society, the higher is the aforementioned hope in the girls who have just reached the stage of internal orientation and desire for the opposite sex, and consequently, they will accept toleration more easily. But, with the increase in conventional marriage age for the female gender, this hope in girls will decrease and it would be difficult for them to tolerate this situation.

At first, with the beginning of the sense of desire for the opposite sex and understanding the inner needs, when there is no response from the outside (lack of permanent husband as well as unconventionality of early marriages) to fulfill them, some girls will look for other alternative which have the closest similarity to the state of marriage so that they meet their needs by it. So, having a romantic relationship with an opposite sex before the marriage most resembles the marriage and can serve as an anesthetic for some of these needs. It is obvious that the higher the gap between the beginning of these needs and the conventional marriage age, the easier the justification of having a boyfriend would be.

✓ Due to the lack of stability and sufficient commitments from the two parties in romantic relationships, it is possible that a woman may experience several romantic relationships before marriage; and this can lead to emotional and mental traumas, increased skepticism of opposite genders towards each other, and reduced commitment and emotional belongingness in women and etc.

Prophet Mohammad (P.B.U.H): "O people, Gabriel brought the message of the God that maiden girls are like fruits of trees. When the fruit is ripe, there is no choice but to pick it, otherwise the sun will make it rotten and the wind (air) will change its color. Veritably, when the maidens understand what the women understand (i.e. the emotional and sexual desires), then there is no choice than to marry otherwise they would not be safe from corruption and immorality (Al- Kafi, Volume. 5).

4 –increase in showing off: Since, in romantic relationships and marriage, usually, it is the male gender who selects and the female gender is the selectee, this causes some of the girls and single women in whom the feeling of desire and inclination towards the opposite sex has been awakened, to want to apply all their capabilities to become more attractive and soon be chosen by the male gender. Since, seeing is one of the main factors by which the male gender gets stimulated, it is apparent that the female genders' appearance (face, body and clothes) is considered as the first means of attracting men and creating the inclination towards those girls in them.

Therefore, the beginning of desire for the opposite sex can be one of the main factors in creation of the motive for self displaying of the girls and single women. Increase in the length of 'waiting time for marriage' and the existence of other female rivals will enhance the aforementioned factor, and not only the single men will be aroused, but also it would make the grounds for arousal of the married men.

Moreover, an increased number of girls and single women and their showing off would cause some of the married women, too, to enter this competition cycle by enhancing their attractiveness; the married women do so because they fear that their husband may divert his attention from them to other women (and they want to prevent this from happening).

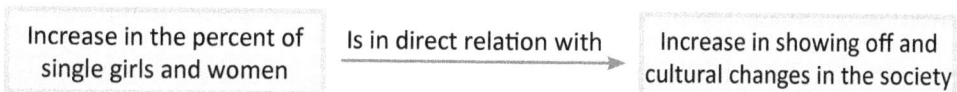

Increase in the percent of single girls and women	Is in direct relation with →	Increase in showing off and cultural changes in the society

5- Family problems: obviously, the increased number of girls and single women intensifies the probability of married men's secret romantic relationships.

Also, with the growth of this kind of relationships in the society, the percentage of the wives' awareness of their husbands' relationships will increase, too. Then, due to anti-conventionality of sharing the husband and difficulty of its acceptance by women, one of the following negative cases will emerge:

- Retaliation: few wives would react to this by doing the same behavior that their husbands have done and by violating the marriage commitments, they will retaliate against their husband's behavior. This is while this kind of behavior is in conflict with their spirit, even though; it is used as a quick reaction.

- File for divorce: due to emergence of distrust and lack of the required motivation, etc, some of them will be disappointed at the continuation of the shared life and would get a divorce.

- The feeling of sadness and dejection: due to the women's natural contradiction with retaliation and not seeing any use in doing counteractive reaction, this way would not be chosen. Also, because of various reasons such as loving the husband and children and not seeing any better future in getting a divorce, etc, divorce would not be considered as a suitable solution. Hence, the most reasonable option is to continue the marital life. However, this matter would stick in their minds as a bitter situation and would lead to emotional problems.

6- Reduced tendency of some men toward getting married at proper time: different issues such as financial qualification, mental and physical qualifications, et cetera contribute to the men's ability or disability in establishing a new family.

Other than the above mentioned factors, there are also some other effective factors in decreasing the men's motivation for marriage while they have the required preliminary conditions for marriage; factors such as the mental effects of increased divorce rates, propensity for indolence and irresponsibility, unusual expectations, etc are some of these disincentives.

One of the most important disincentives is the easy access to the single girls and women for romantic friendship; certainly, increase in their number plays a key role in formation of this phenomenon.

7- Women's commodification and the fading of their human identity: surely, by gradual increase in the number of girls and single women, the tendency toward establishing short-term romantic relationships among single and married men in the society would increase, too.

So, with the growing number of the men seeking this kind of relationship, financial goals have been strongly enhanced in some girls and single women in proportion to their other objectives, and this has led to the formation of a pecuniary market in which the woman's body is offered as a commodity for exchange and money making.

At first, each woman acts individually, but with increase in the number of these women and profitability of this market, it is seen that some other people collect, organize, recruit, and exploit them in their own grouping.

The main negative repercussion of woman's commodification is infringement of the female gender's right which is accompanied by events like trafficking of girls and women to be recruited in these places.

Also, in some regions in which there is legal equality between men and women, the activity of such centers has been legal (and without any limitation for entry of the married men). This demonstrates that the women's legal rights are ignored after their marriage.

8- Increased rate of abortion: undoubtedly, the phenomenon of abortion is considered as one of the events part of which is related to the lack of polygyny and the growth of short-term romantic relationships. This issue can be connected with the increasing number of the aforementioned relationships and consequently the higher probability of unwanted pregnancies (pregnancies at younger ages friendships, in particular) as well as lack of legal and moral conditions in temporary relationships in comparison to the permanent marriages which entail more commitment and force to accept the responsibility of a child.

9- Sustainability and transferability of negative effects to the future: if new men entrants just marry to new women entrants, over time and with the elimination of surplus single women, these inappropriate effects would disappear. But due to the exchanges made between the two groups of the new women entrants to the marriage arena and the surplus single women, the surplus single women's set continuously replaces an old member with a new one and causes these effects to continue.

This is particularly important when the population growth rate is zero. Although, apparently the conditions for the formation of surplus single women are ended, because of the aforementioned exchanges, the conditions for an increase in the number of women and its rising effects (that have been generated in the positive population growth period), would be transferred to the zero population growth period and continue in the society.

10- Other phenomena such as the girls' running away from home, prevalence of sexually transmitted diseases (HPV, HIV,...), the government's paying the expense of spouseless women, increase of fortunetelling, tendency toward animals, higher amount of dowry (due to fear of less likelihood of remarriage after divorce), etc. are directly or indirectly associated with this issue.

Chapter 5:
Complementary Steps of Implementing Polygyny

It was seen that due to the combination of a positive marriage age gap with a positive population growth, the conditions for the relative increase in the number of single women seeking marriage in comparison to single men have existed throughout time. In addition, the inherent tendency of men toward women revealed that polygyny was common in early human communities. So, polygyny is not Islam's invention and innovation, but has been limited and regulated by some constraints to preserve the women's necessary rights; this point has been explicitly referred to in the third verse of the Nisa Surah:

> ... Then marry other woman of your choice, two or three or four; but if you fear that you shall not be able to deal justly (with them), then only marry one free woman or choose from among the captives and slave girls that you own; that is more suitable to prevent you from doing injustice (Nisa surah, Verse 3)[1].

Thus, it can be inferred that in this case Islam has considered and ordered justice as the main condition for men.

---

1. فَانكِحُواْ مَا طَابَ لَكُم مِّنَ النِّسَاء مَثْنَى وَثُلَاثَ وَرُبَاعَ فَإِنْ خِفْتُمْ أَلاَّ تَعْدِلُواْ فَوَاحِدَةً أَوْ مَا مَلَكَتْ أَيْمَانُكُمْ ذَلِكَ أَدْنَى أَلاَّ تَعُولُواْ

Having the Required Justice (Alimony and Sex):

Some legal issues emerge in any marriage between a man and a woman by which the parties are committed to respect and implement the legal right of the other. Accordingly, the wife has some rights, related to her primary needs including financial, emotional, and sexual needs in the family system which the husband is obliged to meet.

Therefore, every man who marries is responsible to meet these needs; if he doesn't have the ability to provide these needs fairly, then he shouldn't marry. This is closer to justice and avoidance of oppressing the woman.

If a man intends to get married once more, he must surely assess that aside from being fair and not oppressing his prior wife or wives, whether he is legally capable to take on responsibility of a new wife's rights?

In the case that he realistically feels the ability to meet these needs in himself, the financial needs in particular, he is allowed to remarry; otherwise, he is responsible for his wife or wives and is accountable in front of god.

> Prophet Mohammad (P.B.U.H): If a man is married to two women
> and behaves unfairly towards them, he is resurrected in the Judgment
> Day, with a lost body (Nahj Al Fasaht, Hadith 234).

On the other hand, a single woman who wants to enter a married man's life by marriage must properly evaluate the man's abilities and see whether he is capable of observing her legal right as a wife without exerting any oppression and injustice toward his other wife or wives. Above all, she should not start a life with him if he has no financial qualifications.

In addition, as far as sexual relation is concerned, the Islamic scholars have determined four-night criterion such that if a man is married to four women, each night is dedicated to one of them; if he is married to less than four women, each ones' right will be one of these four nights and the other nights belong to the man himself.

Justice in Affection:

Based on the physical and behavioral characteristics of the wives, they will be loved differently by their husband. This issue, as an involuntary force, directly affects the man's behavior in practice leading to imbalance in his behavior.

Although, the forces of God-fearing and avoiding oppression have been considered as effective preventive measures, in practice, the husband's behavior is the resultant of the two aforementioned forces and he is unable to behave toward his wives evenly.

Finally, Islam has offered a permissible range of difference in the husbands' practical behavior toward their wives which should not be contravened.

Therefore, by defining a red line to avoid going to extremes, in Islam the man is ordered not to be indifferent to fulfilling the marital and sexual rights of the wife whom he loves less, as if she has no husband.

> You will never be able to regard perfect justice (concerning love and affection) among your wives even if it is your serious desire; so do not incline too much to one of them, so as to leave her (the other one)

hanging (meaning suspense as if she is not a widow nor has a husband);

and if you establish a peaceful relationship and employ piety (know that)

verily, Allah is the merciful forgiving (Nisa Surah, Verse 129) [1].

Being aware of the impossibility of equality in their husband's behavior, the wives can help to reduce this behavioral difference by improving their behavioral characteristics (which impacts the husband's love and affection for them). Also the husband must properly manage among his wives by observing some points like not provoking the sense of being compared in his wives.

Men's Encouragement:

After seeking the permission from the married women, the next stage for legalizing the polygyny is the adequate justice in men (in particular, the sufficient financial ability to lead two or more families). It is evident that in any time, a limited number of men have the required financial ability to implement polygyny as appropriate opportunities.

Furthermore, since with polygyny the men's responsibilities would increase in comparison to monogamy; and this responsibility taking may benefit and improve the society; hence, the moral health of the society is dependent and indebted to these people.

Thus, it is required to stimulate and direct them from relations with less responsibility toward admitting polygyny in such a way that not only would they not be indifferent toward this issue, but also they would become

---

1. وَلَن تَسْتَطِيعُواْ أَن تَعْدِلُواْ بَيْنَ النِّسَاء وَلَوْ حَرَصْتُمْ فَلاَ تَمِيلُواْ كُلَّ الْمَيْلِ فَتَذَرُوهَا كَالْمُعَلَّقَةِ وَإِن تُصْلِحُواْ وَتَتَّقُواْ فَإِنَّ اللهَ كَانَ غَفُورًا رَّحِيمًا

interested in doing it. Therefore, the next step taken by God for implementing the aforementioned goal is encouraging and persuading the capable men to polygyny which was initially inspired by practical behaviors of the Prophet (P.B.U.H) and Imams (AS).

In addition, according to the third verse of Nisa Surah in which the first suggested number by God for men's marriage is 2; it can be stated that not only the married men are allowed to do so, but also they are encouraged provided that they have the capability and required qualifications for polygyny. In other words, Islam has based the men's marriage on polygyny; unless lacking the required conditions, monogamy is advised.

Further, by relying on the various recommendations for meeting the other people's needs including marriage as one of the most important needs, it can be said that there is another ground to encourage the competent men to implement polygyny.

Besides the above mentioned incentives, there are also other motives such as having more children and /or actualizing the potential management and leadership abilities and etc, which encourage men to polygyny and exist in them as an internal motivation.

Consolidation and Creation of a Culture by Using a Model:

Certainly, the presence of valued people with social popularity especially as the implementers and operators of an act can be remarkably effective for proper training, valuation, and finally conventionalization of an issue throughout the society.

Therefore, one of the divine steps taken is to create a culture for eliminating the wrong beliefs around the issue of polygyny. These beliefs are as follows:

• Monogamy is the evidence of loyalty; whereas, polygyny is the evidence of disloyalty;

• A single woman is merely allowed to marry a single man;

• The proposal of a married man to a single woman is an indecent act.

All of these beliefs are to devalue and ultimately misrepresent and reject polygyny; whereas, the implementation of it by the Prophet Muhammad (P.B.U.H), the Imams (A.S) and their companions, not only encouraged polygyny, but also stabilized and valued it forever.

Chapter 6:
Understanding the Forces

According to the fact that over time some percent of the women remain single, it can be indicated that the following measures have been taken by God to prevent the outcomes of this phenomenon:

1-Creation of the man with characteristics of physical possessiveness and polygyny

2-seeking permission from the married women to share their husband and turning this permission to a right for single women

3-Determining the required qualifications for men's remarriage, especially the adequate financial ability

4-Encouraging qualified men to take on more responsibilities

5-Consolidating and creating the culture of polygyny by religious leaders

Then, the next divine measure is making known the forces among the women which impact their making decision on this issue. These forces are both for and against acceptance of polygyny and play a significant role in this matter.

Materialism (Worldliness):

As it is known, human being has a divine spirit which naturally has the propensity to worship God. In addition, since s/he is born in this world and has a physical aspect, necessarily s/he requires some inherent desires and instincts for his mundane affairs.

Thus, human being's involvement in mundane affairs gradually moves him/her far away from his/ her divine nature and a new mundane image of self is created in his/ her mind; the result is interest in materialistic affairs and attachment to them.

Therefore, materialism (loving and attaching extravagant importance to mundane affairs would lead to disbelief in God and the Judgment Day; this would also nurture some beliefs such as self-interest and egotism); strong tendency toward self-interest and egotism would not only deviate human beings from the divine way and faith in the main life after death, but also would enhance some attributes such as greed, envy, and selfishness in them; these attributes are considered as the origin of oppression, corruption, and infringement of others' rights ; they would also bring some personal problems such as grief and sorrow for the person.

Imam Ali (p. b. u. h): "Interest in the world is one of the biggest errors. If you love God, remove any worldly love from your heart. Indeed, you would never meet the Exalted God while you have the love for this world; nothing would prevent you from meeting God save the affection for this world. Love for the world is the origin of seditions and the root of distress. It corrupts the mind, makes the heart deaf to wisdom and causes painful torture. (Mustadrakal-

Wasā'il, Vol. 331/2)

Thus, in order to avoid materialism which results in deviating from the divine way, violating the others' right and wanting to achieve materialistic worlds at any cost (even with oppression), God has limited the human's materialism through some religious orders and principles and has asked the humans to act according to them in order not to immerse themselves in mundane affairs, control and inhibit unappealing traits of greed, jealousy, and selfishness in themselves.

Therefore, enduring the difficulties and pressures from confrontation of the two forces i.e. the force of surrendering before God's demand and the force of mundane tendencies, would pave a proper ground for enhancing the belief in God and measuring human being's obedience to God, in addition to abstaining from oppression and establishing the social justice; this matter is the main philosophy of religion's orders and commandments.

Women's Materialism:

Although, materialism exists among the men and women, the intrinsic factors causing the formations of this interest differs and this is because of their gender; and consequently, they make use of different strategies in fighting with materialism and are tested on this matter differently.

Since humans struggle for life and development, the male gender is equipped with the physical possessiveness characteristic which provides him inherent potential to achieve and enhance physical, financial, and materialistic properties.

In spite of the efficiency of this inherent natural tendency, if he goes to extremes in this regard and does not control this tendency, it will turn into the male gender materialism which not only deters him from the divine way, but also infringes on others' rights.

Therefore, commandments such as Halal[1] living, not violating people's right (through robbery, overcharging, hoarding, usury, bribery, refusal of paying Zakat[2] and Khums[3], etc.) and respecting others' Nāmūs[4] all have been determined for the male gender as the means of monitoring the Nafs (Soul) and fighting with materialism, and also enhancing the belief in God and the Judgment Day, abiding by and acting upon which would lead to social justice as well.

On the other hand, the societies' survival directly depends on the existence of healthy families. So, on the contrary to male gender, the female gender has been created as an emotional and interaction-orientated being; whereby, the woman's inherent potential is to attract a man, establish an emotional relationship with him and win his heart.

The most important result of the woman's emotional belongingness, is

---

1. Halāl or is any object or an action which is permissible to use or engage in, according to Islamic law.
2. Zakāt, «that which purifies», is a form of obligatory alms-giving and religious tax in Islam
3. In Islamic tradition, Khums refers to the historically required religious obligation of Muslim people to pay one-fifth of «the earned profit» this tax was paid to the Caliph or Sultan, representing the state of Islam
4. Nāmūs is the Arabic word of a concept of an ethical category, a virtue, in Middle Eastern patriarchal character. Literally translated as «virtue», it is now more popularly used in a strong gender-specific context of relations within a family described in terms of honor, attention, respect, responsibility, and modesty. The concept of namus in respect to sexual integrity of family members is an ancient, exclusively cultural concept which predates Islam, Judaism, and Christianity.

the tendency to love the husband, making her do all her best (like committing herself to her husband and being loyal to him) in order to achieve the aforementioned objective.

In fact, the most positive impact of this tendency and belongingness will be gaining the husbands' permanent support as well as stabilization and survival of the family, the absence of which may lead to either divorce or a situation of indifference.

But, God has confirmed polygyny so that the inherent inclination of the female gender does not lead to her materialism and has asked her not to deviate from the divine way and not to get attached to the mortal world (the primary cause of polygyny), by accepting polygyny; and moreover, to control and inhibit the internal factor that deprives the single surplus women from marriage (the secondary cause of polygyny).

Thus, by enduring the difficulties and pressures from confrontation of the two forces i.e. the force of emotional acquisition seeking, and the force of obedience to God's demand, the former leading to sensual pleasure of fulfilling the husband's needs and the latter resulting in fulfilling the husband' needs for God's satisfaction; in addition to avoiding oppression and bringing social justice, a proper ground will be provided to measure and enhance the belief in God, as well. This issue is the main philosophy of some principles such as polygyny.

(As this trial is centered on determining the amount of woman's submission to God, polygyny has not been considered obligatory for men in Islam).

The Inner Influential Force Opposing Polygyny:

As it was previously mentioned, the woman's sensitivity to her husband is different from the man's sensitivity to his wife. The former is caused by emotional acquisition seeking inherent in the females' nature; whereas, the latter is caused by the physical possessiveness inherent in the males' nature.

It is obvious that these two forces are equally beneficial for the family, and they both play a key role in reaching the important goal of "maintaining the family's survival"; the former by creating the tendency to love the husband and be loyal to him in woman (the emotional belongingness attribute), and the latter by creating the inclination toward acquisition and retention of the wife as possession territory in men. (Attribute of Qeyrat[1]).

But, regarding the social effectiveness and reaching the state of "establishment of balance between the number of men and women seeking marriage" they function differently.

Therefore, in case of relative increase in the number of men to women, the men's physical possessiveness force would lead to the emergence of the most severe and violent physical behaviors from them for the purpose of permanent physical repulsion or elimination of their rivals, by doing so, the balance between supply and request in marriage will be spontaneously guaranteed.

But, in the case of relative increase in the numbers of women to men, such a behavior is not seen from the female gender. This indicates the difference

---

1. Qeyrat is the Arabic word of a concept of an ethical category, a virtue, in Middle Eastern patriarchal character. Literally translated as "Zealotry", here it is more popularly used in a strong gender-specific context of relations within a family described in terms of honor and dignity.

between the nature and intensity of the two aforementioned forces. In other words, neither the woman's sensitivity to her husband is a kind of physical possessiveness force or Qeyrat nor the man's sensitivity to his wife is a kind of emotional belongingness force (signs of which are the sentences such as I am only for you and belong to you).

***

On the other hand, although physical possessiveness force (Qeyrat) does not exist in woman, the emotional acquisition seeking force makes the wife sensitive toward her husband and expects him to only love her and pay attention to her. Moreover, this sense causes ego comparison in the wife and she expects the husband to be loyal to her and she regards her husband's emotional belongingness behavior as a symbol of love and passion.

So, she will be irritated once her husband wants to love another woman. Unlike the male gender, the woman's dissatisfaction is not due to the ignorance of the physical possessiveness territory by 'another single woman'.

But her main dissatisfaction is with 'her husband'. Because in the woman's view, the husband must have only loved her and not express his love for another woman, too.

The Jealousy Force:

The most powerful major factor in causing the opposition of married women to polygyny is the activation of jealousy in them.

Once the wife is informed of her husband's showing affection for another woman, should she seek to achieve her ultimate goal that is having all of the man's attention, she must prevent the husband from paying attention to another woman and practically try to do so. Since this matter is combined with turning away from goodness and/or hurting the other woman, such behaviors are considered as jealousy.

Imam Baqir (p. b. u. h): Qeyrat in women is the sign of jealousy and jealousy is the root of Kufr [1]. *When the women show Qeyrat, they get angry and when they get angry, they begin to disobey; this is not the case with the Muslim women (who have surrendered to God) (Al-Kafi, Volume 5, p. 505, Hadith. 4).*

Imam Ali (p. b. u. h): Women's Qeyrat indicates kufr (disbelief in God); whereas, the men's Qeyrat is suggestive of their faith in God (Nahj Al-Balaghah, Hikmah. 124).

Imam Sadiq (p. b. u. h): The Most High God has not endowed the women with Qeyrat (or the force of territory acquisition and preservation); only the incompetent women envy [2], *not the Muslim women! The Generous God would not bestow the women with Qeyrat on the one hand; and allow the men to marry more than one woman (up to three other women) legitimately, on the other hand. Indeed, God has bestowed only the men with Qeyrat (physical possessiveness force). Hence, men are allowed to marry up to four women; whereas, women are only allowed to be married to their husband. Thus, the woman wanting another man besides her husband is referred to as adulterer (Al- Kafi, Volume. 5, p. 505, Hadith. 1, 2)*

***

---

1. Kufr is the term which describes disbelief or denial.
2. As concerns the women, Qeyrat mostly equals the attribute of envy

Effective Internal Forces in Favor of Polygyny:

Although the force of jealousy is at the service of Nafs[1] and is intolerant of polygyny, there are still other effective forces in controlling and neutralizing jealousy which are as follows:

1. The Force of Gaining Profit and Rejecting the Loss in Hereafter Life

Certainly, obeying God's commands is somewhat difficult for human beings because they are not in line with the mundane interests. But when the person believes in God and the main life after death, it would be easier for him/ her to detach from worldly affairs for the purpose of gaining some benefits such as God's satisfaction and entering Paradise s/he would tolerate the difficulty of some divine rules.

So, the last divine step is to make known the negative factor in opposing the Polygyny (i.e. jealousy) and encourage the women to accept polygyny through promising great rewards.

> *Prophet Mohammad (p. b. u. h): There are three groups of women who are immune from grave tortures (the mental pressures exerted on human beings from the moment of death until the day of Resurrection) and will be resurrected together with Fatimah (my beloved daughter). The woman who tolerates her husband's other wives, the woman who puts up with her husband's indigence, and the woman who keeps her patience with her husband's petulancy (Wasā'il al-Shī'a, Vol. 21, p. 285).*

> *Prophet Mohammad (P.B.U.H): The woman who tolerates her husband's Qeyrat (and polygyny) will be granted the remuneration of*

---

1. Nafs is an Arabic word occurring in the Qur'an and means self, psyche ego or soul

martyr, (the one who fights and gets killed for God's sake). (Mustadrakal-

Wasā'il l, Vol. 14, p. 237) {'Ilal al-sharāyi', Vol. 1, p. 249}

2. The Force of Gaining Profit and Rejecting the Worldly Loss and the Force of Humanity

Even though it is obligatory for human beings to accept the divine commands even when there is no rational reason their accompaniment with reasons emphasizing their necessity and benefit, can make accepting the commandments easier. Furthermore, the inherent humanity force, altruism, and recognizing affairs such as the superiority of collective interests over personal interests in establishing the social justice will make some activities more valuable for human beings.

Surely, every woman inherently recognizes that marriage, reduction in the women's marriage age, and

establishment of balance in the society is a good phenomenon, contrariwise, women's singleness as well as increase in their marriage age which is along with gradual cultural changes (negative) in the society, are devaluing phenomena. Thus, stimulating the people's sense of responsibility for the society's good or bad events which may affect themselves or their relatives can be effective in encouraging them to accept and revive the polygyny.

Prophet Mohammad (P.B.U.H): You all are the guardian (of the society) and are all responsible towards the citizens (Bihār al-Anwār, Vol. 72, p. 38).

3. Understanding the Ugliness of Violating the Commitment:

It was said that one of the women's rights in the Islamic system is that they are allowed to be the second, the third, or the fourth wife (referring to men's polygyny).

On the other hand, the marriage of a woman according to the standards of Islamic model means that she has accepted all the women's Islamic rights including alimony, dowry as well as polygyny. Hence, rebutting the undesired parts and approving the desired parts of a religion (which this selective acceptance of preferred points is seen in both the Islamic model and the equality model), is in conflict with the woman's commitment regarding the acceptance of the Muslim men and women's rights and is considered as a self-indulgent behavior. Therefore, the third helpful force on this issue is the sense of commitment and avoidance of perfidy in women.

> *... They say: We believe in some of them and disbelieve in others, intending to adopt a way in between (for themselves) (Nisa Surah, Verse of 150).*[1]

Women's want and Effort for Making the Polygyny a Culture:

Though, God has taken the required proceedings to establish polygyny; eventually, it is the want of the women in a society that will lead to conventionalization of polygyny. Generally, every woman can have two possible views on this issue, the total sum of which would be effective in formation of the norms in a society.

---

١. وَ يَقُولُونَ نُؤْمِنُ بِبَعْضٍ وَ نَكْفُرُ بِبَعْضٍ وَ يُرِيدُونَ أَنْ يَتَّخِذُوا بَيْنَ ذلِكَ سَبِيلاً

The first view is accepting the polygyny and trying to show it as a good issue and revive it in the society. The gradual conventionalization of polygyny, not only would prevent the problems of increased number of single women in the society, but also it would control the jealousy, facilitate the acceptance of polygyny among women and reduce the reactions against it.

The second view is rejection of polygyny which happens when women in line with their severe interest and attachment to the mundane affairs, try to focus their effort on worldly matters related to their gender. It can be said that behaviors like being a good wife and fulfilling all their husband's needs to keep him forever, controlling and monitoring him, creating fear through dishonoring and divorcing him, retaliation, suspicion, etc. all are at the service of achieving this goal.

It is clear that rejecting polygyny as an invidious phenomenon may gradually lead to anti-conventionalization and deletion of polygyny at the society level; and finally, besides the convenience of temporary romantic relations in comparison to marriage responsibilities for competent married men, the challenges of fighting with the convention would lead to reduction in their tendency and steps toward polygyny. On the other hand, the single women and girls have to choose tostay in the unmarried state or enter into short-time romantic relations; moreover, accepting to marry the married men will be also more difficult for them.

In conclusion, when polygyny becomes an anti-norm and over time, neither the women nor the men will seek to marry in this way; the only result is that because of increase in the number of single women, more men will have more various romantic relations with different single women.

Therefore, considering the direct effect of accepting or rejecting polygyny on women's status and the whole society, every woman is somehow responsible and plays a crucial role in building her own society's conditions through selecting any of the two aforementioned alternatives.

… Allah will not change what is in a nation unless they change what is in themselves… (AL-RAD Surah, Verse. 11).[1]

---

١. إنَّ اللَّهَ لا يُغَيِّرُ ما بِقَوْمٍ حَتَّى يُغَيِّرُوا ما بِأَنْفُسِهِمْ ...

Appendix 1:
the number of surplus girls and single women in the world

Table4: The population distribution of men and women in the world in terms of age in 2015 (www.census.gov)							
Age	Number of men	Number of women	Age	Number of men	Number of women	Age	Number of men	Number of women
0	67,177,336	63,164,875	32	55,200,677	53,606,041	64	24,518,979	26,467,493
1	66,377,117	62,394,416	33	56,369,533	54,511,962	65	24,107,103	25,984,127
2	65,938,794	61,900,170	34	52,636,941	50,914,252	66	22,058,791	24,045,204
3	65,552,758	61,468,642	35	52,289,758	50,632,381	67	20,831,598	22,840,557
4	65,021,298	60,906,424	36	51,258,010	49,705,385	68	19,611,139	21,688,197
5	64,597,776	60,462,603	37	50,060,043	48,642,531	69	17,196,282	19,235,690
6	64,243,352	60,077,744	38	49,501,033	48,170,689	70	16,040,039	18,059,389
7	63,891,039	59,686,179	39	49,235,531	48,010,577	71	15,242,355	17,335,752
8	63,284,604	59,070,572	40	49,171,627	48,018,493	72	14,372,355	16,651,547
9	62,849,574	58,606,811	41	49,276,158	48,238,754	73	13,739,140	16,317,235
10	62,690,767	58,412,718	42	49,122,866	48,196,611	74	12,962,130	15,659,174
11	62,431,724	58,174,360	43	48,674,617	47,642,134	75	11,998,814	14,851,633
12	62,056,622	57,829,885	44	48,874,403	47,732,960	76	10,999,729	13,904,474
13	61,783,282	57,583,935	45	47,882,681	47,066,826	77	10,279,759	13,225,025
14	61,665,651	57,472,714	46	47,467,150	46,719,004	78	9,328,139	12,264,703
15	61,469,033	57,327,215	47	45,276,982	44,577,340	79	8,438,971	11,352,743
16	61,291,851	57,210,864	48	43,438,822	43,094,798	80	7,488,546	10,317,376
17	61,269,050	57,288,863	49	43,587,434	43,472,661	81	6,641,675	9,341,776
18	61,254,865	57,377,457	50	42,793,666	42,905,166	82	5,901,384	8,606,989
19	61,366,411	57,558,278	51	42,429,652	42,743,497	83	5,102,947	7,714,370
20	61,455,366	57,768,036	52	42,531,103	42,824,376	84	4,462,422	7,013,105
21	61,120,130	57,653,145	53	36,212,019	37,012,724	85	3,840,439	6,304,851
22	60,764,783	57,474,238	54	33,400,684	34,496,078	86	3,152,934	5,450,515
23	60,792,372	57,640,611	55	33,947,707	34,930,170	87	2,630,697	4,743,642
24	60,955,268	58,016,339	56	32,851,901	33,978,710	88	2,091,114	3,992,828
25	62,711,787	59,534,921	57	34,062,213	35,136,839	89	1,655,206	3,364,897
26	61,433,717	58,800,769	58	32,529,707	33,917,353	90	1,298,527	2,817,596
27	60,661,250	58,246,183	59	31,088,057	32,652,729	91	981,075	2,260,428
28	60,752,586	58,436,597	60	31,004,968	32,524,623	92	727,988	1,783,642
29	58,015,265	55,913,661	61	29,254,494	30,914,804	93	543,866	1,407,349
30	56,325,408	54,357,488	62	27,716,254	29,505,474	94	396,779	1,092,397
31	55,673,198	53,936,122	63	26,537,737	28,369,049	95	273,951	802,697

For the numerical illustration of the combination of positive population growth with positive marriage age gap, which causes the increase in the number of girls and single women, we can use the statistics for the world's population in 2015 (Table 4).

For this purpose and supposing that all the 2.141.127.780 men between the ages of 24 to 95 are married, in the case that different average marriage age gaps are conventional (0, +1, +2, +3, +4, +5, +6 years in which the men's age is equal or greater than the women's age), then the number of surplus girls and single women remaining from each age range in the world would be:

Men's age range	Total number of men at each age range	Average age gap (year)	Women's age range	Total number of women at each age range	Total number of surplus girls and women
(24-95)	2.141.127.780	0	(24-95)	2.185.004.472	43.876.692
(24-95)	2.141.127.780	+1	(23-94)	2.241.842.386	100.714.606
(24-95)	2.141.127.780	+2	(22-93)	2.298.224.227	157.096.447
(24-95)	2.141.127.780	+3	(21-92)	2.354.470.023	213.342.243
(24-95)	2.141.127.780	+4	(20-91)	2.410.454.417	269.326.637
(24-95)	2.141.127.780	+5	(19-90)	2.465.752.276	324.624.496
(24-95)	2.141.127.780	+6	(18-89)	2.520.312.128	379.184.348

For instance, it is seen that considering the average marriage age gap of +5 years for the aforementioned men, roughly speaking, there would be no husband for 324 million women between the ages of 19 to 90 throughout the world and they will remain as surplus single women.

Appendix 2:
Marriage age gap bases

There are various bases for couple's age proportionality and also for determining the appropriate age gap between the man and woman at the time of marriage; each of these bases specifies the kind of girl or woman to whom a man having adequate financial ability is equal and can marry. It is clear that when one of these bases becomes a convention, then the percentage of the marriages taking place based on that basis would be more than the marriages which take place according to other bases in the society. These bases include:

• **The same-age:** once the man has adequate financial ability to afford a married life, he marries a woman as old as himself (Zero age gap state).

• **Puberty age difference:** once the man has adequate financial ability to afford a married life, he marries a girl younger than himself; i.e. the age gap between them equals the average time difference between the puberty in boys and girls (an example of positive age gap)

• **The beginning of desire:** once the man has adequate financial ability to afford a married life, he marries a girl younger than himself who has just reached the stage of heterosexual orientation and desire (another example of the positive age gap).

Since it is probable that each one of the above-mentioned age gaps may become a convention in society, it is necessary to study and compare them in order to make these bases better understood. For this purpose we can devise the criterion: "Women's and girls' waiting time for marriage".

This criterion has been dedicated to study the time length from the very beginning of orientation and desire for the opposite sex until the permanent marriage. Here, since the time matters, the option in which the time length is reduced to the least possible amount has priority over other options.

Once the "puberty difference marriage" becomes a convention in the society (the average age gap between the married couples equals that of the puberty difference in them), after the beginning of desire for the opposite sex in girls, they should wait for a man to reach adequate financial ability. It means that the women's and girls' waiting time for marriage has been dependent on men's financial ability. In this state, because of the above-mentioned dependency, it is obvious that with an increase in the length of time taken for a man to reach the due financial ability, the marriage age in women would increase, too.

Conventionality of the same-age marriages in the society (in which, on average, the couples are the same age), would lengthen this waiting time. Thus, after the beginning of desire for the opposite sex in girls, they should marry the men who are the same age as themselves and also have reached the adequate financial ability.

The last state is when the marriages based on the beginning of desire become a convention. Its advantage over the other two above mentioned states is that in this state, the women's and girls' waiting time for marriage is minimized. So that as soon as the sense of orientation and desire for the opposite sex or husband is awakened in girls, there would be many suitors for them.

Therefore, one might conclude that with conventionality of marriages based on the beginning of desire in the society _in which the couples' age gap is positive_, the women's and girls' waiting time for marriage would be reduce to the smallest possible amount. However, change of the convention to marriages based on the puberty age difference of the couples, and also the same-age marriages (i.e. the marriages with negative age gap) would lengthen this time.

References:

Books:

- holy Quran, Nahj Al-Balaghah, Al-Kafi, Wasāil al-Shīa, Mustadrakal-Wasāil, Bihār al-Anwār, Ilal al-sharāyi', Nahj Al Fasaht

Presentation lecture:

- "The Signs of the Apocalypse". (The Woman of the Apocalypse, 1& 2), Ayat, Seyed Mohammad Hassan

Paper:

- "Why God has endowed women with emotional acquisition sense and in contrast has permitted men to practice polygyny?", Aman allahi, Hassan

www.census.gov/topic/population/international/data/world population summary/ **population by age&...**

******

Relevant News websites:

- www.tabnak.ir

  • The worrying increase in abortions

  • Increase in the marriage of boys to the girls older than them

  • The outstanding statistical difference in the number of old single girls and the divorced women in Iran.

- www.lifesitenews.com/news/russia- may-legalize- polygamy-for-10- million-lonely-women.

- www.aljazeera.net//الجزائر فى فتاه مليون 11 يطارد العنوسه شبح

The ghost of spinsterhood is chasing 11 million girls in Algeria